Baldwinsville Public Library
33 East Genesee Street
Baldwinsville, NY 13027-2575

MAR 2 9 2017

WITHDRAWN

D1397951

Baldwinsville Public Library
33 East Genesee Street
Baldwinsville, NY 13027-2575

BIG PICTURE 📷 SPORTS

Meet the
ATLANTA
FALCONS

BY
ZACK BURGESS

NORWOODHOUSE PRESS

CHICAGO, ILLINOIS

NorwoodHouse Press

P.O. Box 316598 • Chicago, Illinois 60631
For more information about Norwood House Press please visit our website at
www.norwoodhousepress.com or call 866-565-2900.

Photo Credits:
All photos courtesy of Associated Press, except for the following: National Football League (6),
Black Book Partners (7, 15, 18, 22, 23), Topps, Inc. (10 both, 11 top,), McDonald's Corp. (11 middle),
Sports Illustrated for Kids (11 bottom).

Cover Photo: Scott Boehm, Associated Press.

The football memorabilia photographed for this book is part of the authors' collection. The collectibles used
for artistic background purposes in this series were manufactured by many different card companies—
including Bowman, Donruss, Fleer, Leaf, O-Pee-Chee, Pacific, Panini America, Philadelphia Chewing Gum,
Pinnacle, Pro Line, Pro Set, Score, Topps, and Upper Deck—as well as several food brands, including
Crane's, Hostess, Kellogg's, McDonald's and Post.

Designer: Ron Jaffe
Series Editors: Mike Kennedy and Mark Stewart
Project Management: Black Book Partners, LLC.
Editorial Production: Lisa Walsh

LIBRARY OF CONGRESS CATALOGING-IN-PUBLICATION DATA   MAR 2 9 2017
Names: Burgess, Zack.
Title: Meet the Atlanta Falcons / by Zack Burgess.
Description: Chicago, Illinois : Norwood House Press, [2016] | Series: Big
    picture sports | Includes bibliographical references and index.
Identifiers: LCCN 2015025436| ISBN 9781599537351 (Library Edition : alk.
    paper) | ISBN 9781603578387 (eBook)
Subjects: LCSH: Atlanta Falcons (Football team)--History--Juvenile
    literature. | Atlanta Falcons (Football team)--Miscellanea--Juvenile
    literature.
Classification: LCC GV956.A85 B87 2016 | DDC 796.332/6409758231--dc23
LC record available at http://lccn.loc.gov/2015025436

© 2017 by Norwood House Press. All rights reserved.
No part of this book may be reproduced without written permission from the publisher.
The Atlanta Falcons is a registered trademark of Atlanta Falcons Football Club, LLC.
This publication is not affiliated with Atlanta Falcons Football Club, LLC,
The National Football League, or The National Football League Players Association.

288N—072016
Manufactured in the United States of America in North Mankato, Minnesota

CONTENTS

Words in **bold type** are defined on page 24.

The Falcons are a "high-flying" team.

CALL ME A FALCON

A falcon soars through the air with speed and grace. It protects its home with courage. In 1966, the Atlanta Falcons joined the National Football League (NFL). Since then, they have shown how much they have in common with the bird they are named after.

The Falcons have always put exciting teams on the field. They made it to their first Super Bowl in 1999. The Falcons look for great quarterbacks to lead them. Two of the best were **Steve Bartkowski** ● → and Matt Ryan.

Matt Ryan gets ready to throw a pass.

The Georgia Dome has hosted the Super Bowl twice.

Best Seat in the House

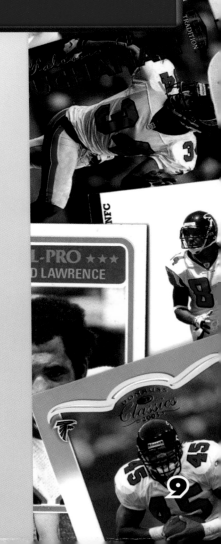

For many years, the Falcons played their home games in an outdoor stadium. In 1992, they moved into the Georgia Dome. In 2015, the team began work on a new stadium. It features a roof that can open and close.

Shoe Box

The trading cards on these pages show some of the best Falcons ever.

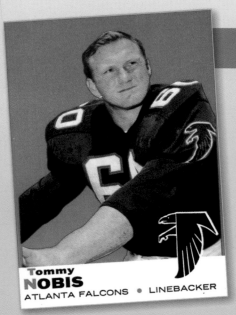

Tommy
NOBIS
ATLANTA FALCONS • LINEBACKER

Tommy Nobis

Linebacker • 1966–1976

Tommy was the Falcons' very first **draft pick**. He was one of the NFL's fastest linebackers.

Claude Humphrey

Defensive End • 1968–1978

Claude was a dangerous pass rusher. He was an **All-Pro** in 1972 and 1973.

FALCONS

CLAUDE HUMPHREY • DE

STEVE BARTKOWSKI

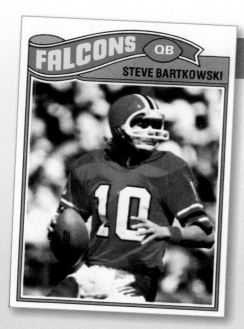

QUARTERBACK · 1975-1985
Steve had one of the most powerful arms in the NFL. In 1980, he led the league in touchdown passes.

DEION SANDERS

CORNERBACK · 1989-1993
Deion stuck to receivers like glue. And no one was more dangerous returning punts and kickoffs.

RODDY WHITE

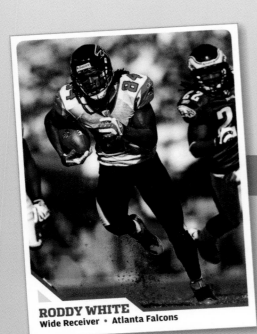

WIDE RECEIVER · FIRST YEAR WITH TEAM: 2005
Roddy led the NFL with 115 catches in 2010. He had 100 receptions the following season.

THE BIG PICTURE

Look at the two photos on page 13. Both appear to be the same. But they are not. There are three differences. Can you spot them?

Answers on page 23.

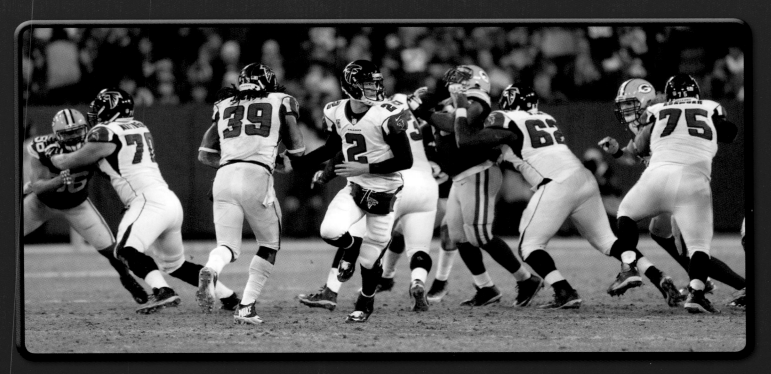

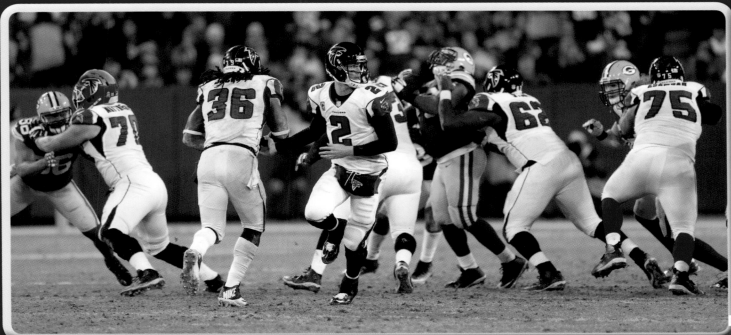

13

TRUE OR FALSE?

Matt Ryan was a star quarterback. Two of these facts about him are **TRUE**. One is **FALSE**. Do you know which is which?

1. Matt threw for a touchdown on his first NFL pass.

2. Matt raises pet falcons between seasons.

3. Matt's nickname is "Matty Ice" because he's so cool under pressure.

Answer on page 23.

Matt Ryan looks for an open teammate.

Julio Jones signs autographs for young Falcons fans.

Go Falcons, Go!

On game day for the Falcons, thousands of fans get to the stadium early. Many go to a place called Falcons Landing. There, they get their faces painted. They watch the Falcons dance team. And they cheer for the college drumline squads.

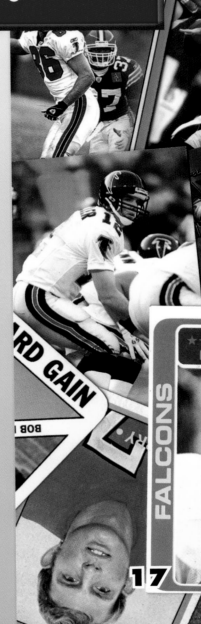

On the Map

Here is a look at where five Falcons were born, along with a fun fact about each.

1 **CHRIS CHANDLER · EVERETT, WASHINGTON**
Chris quarterbacked the Falcons to their first Super Bowl.

2 **TONY GONZALEZ · TORRANCE, CALIFORNIA**
Tony made the **Pro Bowl** his last four seasons
with the Falcons.

3 **MIKE KENN · EVANSTON, ILLINOIS**
Mike holds the Falcons' record with 251 games played.

4 **JEFF VAN NOTE · SOUTH ORANGE, NEW JERSEY**
Jeff was picked to play in the Pro Bowl five times as a Falcon.

5 **MORTEN ANDERSEN · COPENHAGEN, DENMARK**
Morten was an All-Pro for the Falcons in 1995.

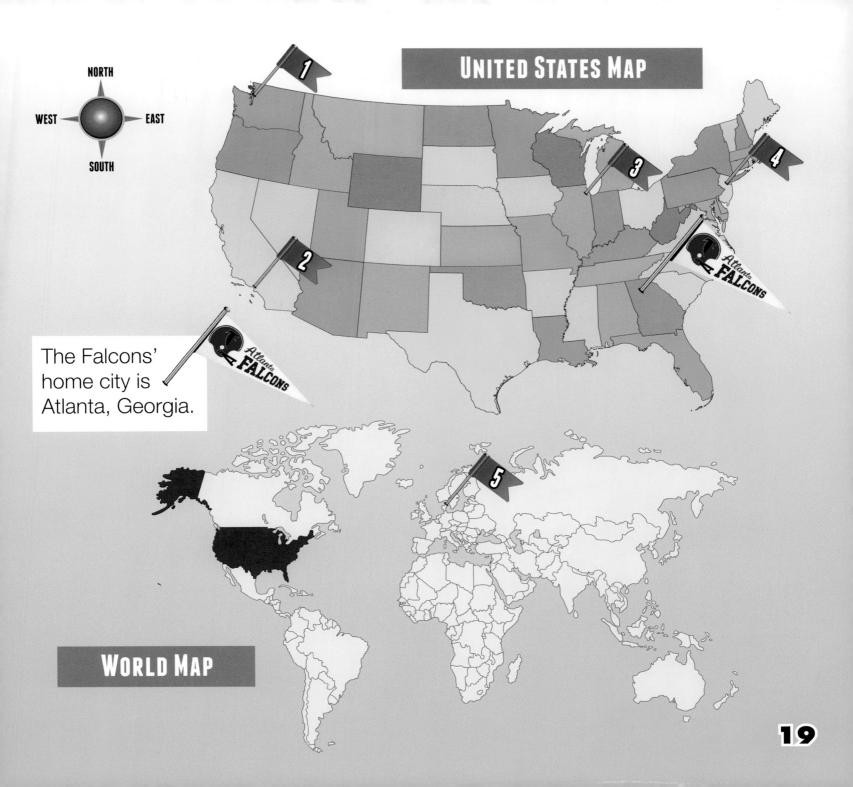

NORTH

WEST ● EAST

SOUTH

1

2

3

4

The Falcons' home city is Atlanta, Georgia.

Atlanta FALCONS

Atlanta FALCONS

5

WORLD MAP

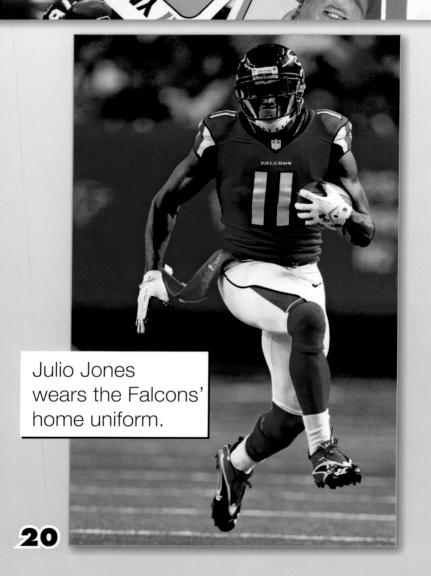

Julio Jones wears the Falcons' home uniform.

Football teams wear different uniforms for home and away games. The Falcons have kept the same colors for their entire history. They have always worn a mix of red, black, and white.

20

Devonta Freeman wears the Falcons' away uniform.

The Falcons' helmet is black. It shows a falcon soaring on each side. The falcon has its talons out, ready to capture its prey.

WE WON!

The Falcons reached the Super Bowl for the first time after the 1998 season. Coach **Dan Reeves** had a heart operation that year. The players and fans hoped he would return to the sidelines. Reeves did, and the Falcons soared through the **playoffs**.

RECORD BOOK

These Falcons set team records.

PASSING YARDS	RECORD
Season: Matt Ryan (2012)	4,719
Career: Matt Ryan	32,757

RUSHING YARDS	RECORD
Season: Jamal Anderson (1998)	1,846
Career: **Gerald Riggs**	6,631

TOUCHDOWN CATCHES	RECORD
Season: Andre Rison (1993)	15
Career: Roddy White	63

ANSWERS FOR THE BIG PICTURE
#70's helmet changed to red, #39 changed to #36, and #75's socks changed to red.

ANSWER FOR TRUE AND FALSE
#2 is false. Matt does not raise pet falcons between seasons.

FOOTBALL WORDS

INDEX

All-Pro
An honor given to the best NFL player at each position.

Draft Pick
A player selected during the NFL's meeting each spring.

Playoffs
The games played after the regular season that decide which teams will play in the Super Bowl.

Pro Bowl
The NFL's annual all-star game.

Photos are on **BOLD** numbered pages.

ABOUT THE AUTHOR

Zack Burgess has been writing about sports for more than 20 years. He has lived all over the country and interviewed lots of All-Pro football players, including Brett Favre, Eddie George, Jerome Bettis, Shannon Sharpe, and Rich Gannon. Zack was the first African American beat writer to cover Major League Baseball when he worked for the *Kansas City Star*.

ABOUT THE FALCONS

Learn more at these websites:

www.atlantafalcons.com • www.profootballhof.com

www.teamspiritextras.com/Overtime/html/falcons.html